A Gift For:

_____

From:

_____

How to Use Your Interactive Story Buddy™ :

1. Activate your Story Buddy by pressing the "On / Off" button on the ear.
2. Read the story aloud in a quiet place. Speak in a clear voice when you see the highlighted phrases.
3. Listen to your Story Buddy respond with several different phrases throughout the book.

Clarity and speed of reading affect the way Abigail™ responds.
She may not always respond to young children.

Watch for even more interactive Story Buddy characters.
For more information, visit us on the Web at Hallmark.com/StoryBuddy.

Copyright © 2011 Hallmark Licensing, LLC

Published by Hallmark Gift Books,
a division of Hallmark Cards, Inc.,
Kansas City, MO 64141
Visit us on the Web at Hallmark.com.

All rights reserved. No part of this publication may be
reproduced, transmitted, or stored in any form or by any
means without the prior written permission of the publisher.

Editors: Emily Osborn and Megan Langford
Art Director: Kevin Swanson
Designer: Mary Eakin
Production Artist: Dan Horton

ISBN: 978-1-59530-360-8
KOB8023
Printed and bound in China
JAN13

I Reply™
TECHNOLOGY

Hallmark's I Reply Technology brings your
Story Buddy™ to life! When you read the
key phrases out loud, your Story Buddy™
gives a variety of responses, so each time you read feels
as magical as the first.

BOOK 2

ABIGAIL
AND
The Tea Party

Hallmark

By Lisa Riggin

Illustrated by
Lynda Calvert-Weyant

Of all the little girls in all the world, there wasn't one
who wanted to grow up as much as Abigail.

Today, Abigail's mom was having a tea party for the
neighborhood ladies, and Abigail would be there, too.
Abigail loved doing grown-up things!

Abigail polished the teapot to help her mom.
She felt so grown-up and asked lots of questions
while she worked.

Should she put her pinkie up when she drank her
tea? Should she curtsy to everyone? Do ladies dunk their
cookies in their tea? There was so much to learn!
Abigail was very, very excited.

Abigail arranged lemon slices in sunny circles
on a plate. Oops! She licked the juice from
her hands. It made her whole face pucker up!

Abigail's mom laughed and said,
"Abigail, is that what ladies do?"

"It's time to get the berries from the backyard."
said Abigail's mom. "I'm really glad to have your
help today."

Abigail ran outside to pick a big basket of berries.
She only ate a few – just to make sure they were
good and sweet!

When she was done, she would help her mom
wash the berries and put them on the table.
Abigail was very, very excited.

At last, everything was ready for the party!
When the doorbell rang, Abigail turned
cartwheels all the way to the front door!

Abigail's mom held back a laugh and asked,
"Abigail, is that what ladies do?"

The ladies looked so beautiful in their big hats and frilly dresses. Old Mrs. Higgenbottom was even wearing gloves!

It didn't matter to Abigail that she wasn't always
sure what everyone was talking about. She had
fun saying, "Oh, yes," and "Isn't that lovely?"
Abigail sounded just like all of the other ladies.

Unfortunately, the tea didn't taste quite as good as Abigail imagined. She put one, two, three, four, five sugar cubes in her cup and stirred. When Abigail looked up, she saw old Mrs. Higgenbottom frowning at her from across the table.

Smiling sheepishly, Abigail tried to sip her tea the proper way.

Then Abigail's eye was caught by the sparkle of the cubes in the sugar bowls. "They look a lot like building blocks," she thought and began to build a sugar cube princess castle.

Old Mrs. Higgenbottom pursed her lips and peered at Abigail with a sour expression. Abigail's rosy cheeks got even rosier as she put all of the sugar cubes back in the bowl.

Abigail tried her best to sit quietly while the ladies talked. She swung her legs back and forth, back and forth until – oops! – a shoe flew off, sailed across the room and scared the cat! Meow!!

"Tsk, tsk, tsk," said Mrs. Higgenbottom, shaking her head. "Abigail, is that what ladies do?"

Except for dropping a spoon and crawling around
on the floor to find it, Abigail felt like she got through
the rest of the tea party in very ladylike fashion.

As the ladies were preparing to leave, Mrs. Higgenbottom glanced out the back window and noticed the berry bushes in the backyard. "Are those the delicious berries we had today?" she asked.

"I picked them," said Abigail. "Would you like to see?" Mrs. Higgenbottom's eyes narrowed. Abigail could feel her cheeks getting warm.

Finally, Mrs. Higgenbottom said, "Yes, young lady, I think I would like that very much." Abigail was very, very excited.

First, Abigail took Mrs. Higgenbottom to the berry bushes to show her where she had picked the berries. Then, she showed her the willow tree where she liked to play house.

When the other ladies had gone, Abigail's mom joined them under the tree. The two of them showed Mrs. Higgenbottom the swing where they'd sit and read together on sunny days.

Abigail smiled at Mrs. Higgenbottom. "I've got
a hula hoop. Want to give it a twirl?"
"Well, I...that is, I never...I mean – why not!"
laughed Mrs. Higgenbottom.
Abigail and her mom took turns showing
Mrs. Higgenbottom how to get the hoop started.
She managed to twirl it twice before it fell to
the ground. All three giggled with delight.
Abigail couldn't help but smile.

"You are a very lucky young lady, Miss Abigail,"
said a tired and happy Mrs. Higgenbottom,
plopping down on the swing. "I look
forward to seeing you at our next tea party."
Abigail sat next to her.

"She'll be there," said Abigail's mom.

Thinking about that made her smile, because
Abigail loved doing grown-up things.

As they swung gently in the breeze, talking and laughing, Abigail looked back at everything she'd done that day.

The tea party was really nice, she thought, and so was this! Abigail beamed with delight.

Did you have fun reading with Abigail™?
We would love to hear from you!

Please send your comments to:
Hallmark Book Feedback
P.O. Box 419034
Mail Drop 215
Kansas City, MO 64141

Or e-mail us at:
booknotes@hallmark.com